Aspects of Geography

General Editors: Keith Clayton and J

Industrial Location

G. Clark
Department of Geography
University of Lancaster

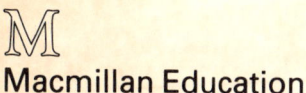

To my aunt

© G. Clark 1983

All rights reserved. No reproduction, copy or transmission of this publication may be made without written permission. No paragraph of this publication may be reproduced, copied or transmitted save with written permission or in accordance with the provisions of the Copyright Act 1956 (as amended). Any person who does any unauthorised act in relation to this publication may be liable to criminal prosecution and civil claims for damages.

First published 1983
Reprinted 1985

Published by
MACMILLAN EDUCATION LTD
Houndmills, Basingstoke, Hampshire RG21 2XS
and London
Companies and representatives
throughout the world

British Library Cataloguing in Publication Data

Clark, G.
  Industrial location, — (Aspects of geography)
  1. Industries, Location of
   I. Title   II. Series
  338.6'042   HC79.D5

ISBN 0-333-34810-9

Typeset by Oxprint Ltd, Oxford
Printed in Hong Kong

Contents

Preface	iv
Introduction	1
Location and production costs	4
Location and sales	12
Government influence	20
The structure of industry	31
The influence of industrialists	38
Conclusion	46
Topics for discussion	49
Further reading	50

Preface

In recent years geography has been changing with great speed. It is not just that the basic facts of geographical distributions are themselves changing, although this of course is happening. It is also that geographers have come to think differently about the significance of geographical distributions and geographical change, about how they study these phenomena and about what topics are worthy of geographical investigation.

Nobody can remain in close touch with the expanding frontier of geographical knowledge at all its points. Accordingly *Aspects of Geography* has been organised as a series of concise reports by writers who are in direct contact with a particular sector of the subject's development. Although the series is aimed in particular at the inquiring A-level student and his teacher, it is hoped that it will also be useful to college and university students as an introduction to the various specialist fields that will be covered.

The location of manufacturing industry is important for governments, for firms and for the public at large because, directly and indirectly, it influences where people want to live and work, and the patterns of freight movements, commuter traffic and population migration associated with the changing distribution of employment. As a result, an understanding of the location of industry has obvious practical relevance. It also has interesting theoretical aspects, since there are optimal industrial locations which can be specified deductively and, too, there are recurring patterns of behaviour by decision-makers which can allow other geographical generalisations to be made.

The location of industry is thus of considerable interest for academic geographers, but in addition it is of the utmost significance for the prosperity of the nation, for broad economic regions within the state, and for smaller areas (for example, the inner districts of large cities). This book provides an effective introduction to this important topic, presented with commendable clarity at a level which should be accessible to the interested layman as well as to the student of geography.

J. H. Johnson
K. M. Clayton

Introduction

Our existence in time is determined for us, but we are largely free to select our location. (A. Lösch, 1954)

How do industrialists select their factories' locations? What criteria do they use and is it a free choice or are they constrained by laws or economic forces? These are the questions to which this book addresses itself.

It is important to try to obtain an understanding of the distribution of manufacturing industry since its location affects not only industrial firms but also local and national governments and those who provide transport services. Location is important for industrial firms since it can influence their profitability and even their survival. From a government's point of view, the distribution of industry contributes to the economic health of the nation, regions and smaller areas like the inner parts of cities. It also influences where people wish to live and hence the public services and housing which should be provided. Manufacturing necessitates goods being carried between factories and then to the final customer, and so the distribution of factories controls the scale and direction of freight traffic. Commuting patterns also are partly moulded by where industry operates. Therefore, there are clear practical benefits for all concerned from explaining the location of industry and predicting or controlling its future location.

In addition to these practical benefits, there is the academic interest in studying how industrialists take decisions about where to establish factories. Geographers often wish to be able to understand industry as a whole. Some try to generalise on the basis of case studies, collecting the common threads and recurring patterns of behaviour and influences – an inductive approach. Others presuppose that a small number of 'factors' are chiefly responsible for the location of firms. They study the extent to which the distribution of industry in the real world corresponds to that predicted by the operation of these factors alone – a deductive approach. Both approaches can be useful: the inductive particularly so at the scale of the individual company or the small area, and the deductive for whole countries or industrial sectors. Examples of both approaches will be described in this book.

The study of the location of industry is as much historical geography as it is economic geography. It must be remembered that explanations should be cast in terms of the conditions operating at the time each factory was established. How the firm survived at a place is a separate question which widens the study. Why did that firm change its product, methods and marketing in order to survive rather than change its location? Only a minority of factories change their positions since this is an expensive process. The initial decision on where to locate is therefore very important.

Much work in industrial geography has been concerned with the best location for industry rather than its actual distribution. If the optimal location for each industry could be specified, one could take steps to improve the distribution of firms for the benefit of businessmen and governments. Several theories which show where industry ideally ought to locate – the so-called normative theories of location – will be described in this book.

> *The real duty of the economist is not to explain our sorry reality, but to improve it. The question of the best location is far more dignified than determination of the actual one.*
> (A. Lösch, 1954)

The difficulty arises in specifying where the optimum is, since there are several 'best' locations depending on which criterion is being considered. The best location for industry's short-term profitability need not be the same as for long-term profitability. The best locations for maximum sales and maximum profits may well be in different places. A government concerned with regional policy will define the optimum distribution of industry differently from an entrepreneur wishing to set up one factory. There are many 'best' locations depending on who is being considered, the scale of the study and the objective to be achieved. Indeed, even if an optimum location could be found, its position would only be fixed if costs, prices, technology and customer preferences were definitely known and never changed. These are such unlikely conditions that the concept of the optimum location is a will-o'-the-wisp however it is defined, flitting unpredictably across the economic landscape.

While it is often convenient to discuss industry, this can be misleading if it implies that all industrial sectors, let alone all firms, are similar. Each firm views space and distance differently. Some firms need many raw materials, others need plenty of land and others require rapid access to information. The sort of location best suited to each will clearly be different. Some firms are trying to sell as much as possible of a low-cost product, while others are tapping a smaller high-quality market. Distance means less to a large firm which has a national monopoly of a market than it does to a small firm in a fiercely competitive industry. Location is also affected by external influences like governments. Sometimes firms are allowed to operate wherever they wish, and in other circumstances they are guided or even forced to particular places in order to protect the public from pollution or to achieve a balance of economic growth between regions. The differences between firms and within industrial sectors is a theme which will recur several times in this book.

Consequently the location of industry is a complex subject at whatever scale it is approached, but it is one where many insights have already been gained. The distribution of industry is not to be explained by any single factor, like transport costs, but equally it is neither haphazard, nor unpredictable. This book sets out to show how industrialists, and principally those in the developed world, have selected where to manufacture our material needs and exports. Its aim is to demonstrate both the recurring patterns in the process and in the distribution of industry today, as well as the new trends emerging as the Western economies evolve.

Location and production costs

A number of writers have suggested that production costs play a major part in the choice of a site by industrial firms and that industrial location can be explained with reference to the geography of production costs. It is argued that production costs vary considerably from place to place and that firms can raise their profitability by establishing their factories where production costs are lowest.

One of the earliest researchers to study variations in production costs was Alfred Weber in his major work published in 1909. He divided production costs into various components which he analysed separately. Initially he examined transport costs to see what effect they had on the location of firms. He concluded that their effect depended on four factors. The first is the weight/volume ratio of the raw materials being used. Cement, which is a heavy, bulky, low-value product, is affected by transport costs more severely than a light, high-value product like diamonds. The second factor is whether or not the raw material tends to lose weight during manufacture – iron ore compared with crude oil, for example. The third factor is whether the raw material is localised in occurrence (a mineral ore, for example) or is found in most places, like water. Localised occurrence attracts manufacturing firms more than do places with a common raw material. Finally, the volume of raw materials will affect their locational pull. Therefore a low-value, localised raw material which loses weight during manufacture and is required in large quantities will tend to attract the factories of firms needing to use this raw material in their manufacturing. Weber noted how one could calculate the exact point where total transport costs were minimised and hence where a factory should be located, all other things being equal. However, the calculation in the form put forward by Weber is of little practical or theoretical use. It ignores all the other aspects of production costs – wage rates and factory rents, for example – and the calculations are straightforward with transport costs a simple multiple of the distance travelled, which usually they are not. It also assumes that all sources of supply, markets, transport costs and technology are constant, which is clearly unrealistic. Weber's study of transport costs as an influence on industrial location is only useful in general terms. It helps explain the location of those industries where the transport bill is a major component of the cost of production and is a component which varies considerably from place to place. Industries in this category include cement manufacture, iron works, pulp mills and sugar-beet refineries. However, Chisholm noted that in 1963 transport costs accounted for less than 5 per cent of total production costs for 57 per cent of British firms and that at least two-thirds of these costs were caused by loading and unloading the goods, a cost which does not vary however far goods are carried. Transporting goods is cheaper than ever before and so the importance of transport costs is now much diminished. Even in industries such as steel manufacture, the increasing use of scrap metal, the partial purification of the ore before transport and cheaper methods of carriage, such as larger ships, have reduced the importance of transport in the overall cost of making steel. Iron ore and coal can now be carried economically from Australia to Japan, the USA or Europe, for example.

Weber was, of course, aware that other costs than transport were involved in manufacturing. The wages and salaries of employees often form the major outgoing for many firms today. Weber noted that cheap-labour locations might attract industry provided the savings on the wage bill were greater than any additional transport costs involved. The importance of low labour costs is evident from the shift in the textile industry from developed countries to the Third World. Industries such as the assembly of electronic components and electrical equipment which are labour-intensive and can use workers with limited training are likely to seek out cheap-labour locations. Should a cheap-labour location experience faster wage inflation than its rivals, as Hong Kong has, its industrial structure is likely to evolve towards less labour-intensive sectors. The tendency in developed countries has been for the variation in wages from region to region to narrow somewhat with the spread of trade union membership and national wage agreements. This has reduced the locational pull of particular places within a country although low wages have been used to explain the rapid industrialisation of the southern states of the USA since 1960. Higher wage rates can, of course, be counteracted by better technology and management which raise the productivity of employees and reduce the labour component in each item produced. This can give a new lease of life to old-established industries and can let high-wage regions compete with cheaper locations where the work force does not have the skills to use more complex technology.

A third element in production costs is the size of the potential market. Many products are cheaper per item when made in large quantities, therefore the size of the potential market is important. A small African country has only a limited market for steel, for example, so even steel transported thousands of miles from the USA, Japan or Europe may be cheaper than the steel produced from a small, local blast-furnace. If the domestic industry does survive it will probably be because of national pride and taxes on imported steel. Otherwise the size of the available market will affect the range of industries a country can support. The formation of large customs unions without industrial tariffs such as the European Community effectively enlarges the European domestic market until it exceeds even that of the USA. This alters where European and American multinational firms locate factories in Europe. Fewer, larger works can satisfy the European market, a trend which is reinforced in those industries where technical advances are continually raising the size of factory at which production costs are at a minimum. Fewer bakeries, for example, can now supply larger markets. This rationalisation of factories is only possible where transport costs are so low, or competition so weak, that the greater total cost of distributing the product from a single factory is more than outweighed by the savings in production costs because of the greater scale of output.

Another way to reduce production costs is to make savings on the cost of the land and premises which the factory will need. This principally affects two types of firm, those needing very cheap premises and those requiring a great deal of land. Very cheap premises are attractive to small and newly established firms which have to devote their limited resources to buying equipment and stocks of raw materials. Cheap premises are usually either small, dilapidated or both. The older parts of cities provide such premises in abundance despite the higher property prices there. Old mills are subdivided and converted to other industrial uses on short leases. Backyards and sheds become small workshops. Inner-city areas provide a useful base for small firms with limited requirements for space.

Firms requiring a lot of space are often very large companies and minimising their land costs usually means a location on the edge of the city where land prices are cheaper and large sites can be obtained. Nearer the city centre, land prices are higher and large sites become difficult to find because of the denser road network and the complexity of landownership. However, what was a peripheral location when a factory was set up may have been engulfed by the city's subsequent expansion until it appears today as an inner-city site. The desirability of a site on the urban fringe has been increased by the growth of assembly-line manufacturing techniques which work most cheaply when the factory is a single-storey building. The multi-storey factory or mill is often not the cheapest architectural layout for current production methods, and so new and long-established firms seeking to expand or redevelop are looking to peripheral locations as the cheapest site.

However, such firms cannot go too far from the city even though land prices may continue to fall the further one goes into the countryside. Although land and labour costs may be higher in the city, a city also provides many savings, collectively called urbanisation economies. It provides a wealth of skills, and easy access to suppliers and customers, particularly when access might be required quickly, which helps reduce the considerable expense of keeping extensive stocks of raw materials. A city also provides from general taxation many services for its population in the way of public transport, housing, roads, water and power supplies. Industrialists can often use these extra services extensively without having to pay the full cost. The Swedish economist Myrdal has suggested that in the early days of industrialisation the expansion of the city as a source of labour and a market was beneficial for further industrial growth. Industrialisation prompted urbanisation of the population which in its turn, as cities grew larger, improved the conditions for industry and attracted it all the more strongly to the city. There was therefore a circular and cumulative relationship between urbanisation and industrialisation, each benefiting from and reinforcing the other.

It can be argued, however, that the savings possible from a city location are no longer as large as they once were. The speed of road transport and the spread of public facilities to smaller towns and rural areas have reduced the need for a city location. Some information can be obtained by telecommunications rather than through face-to-face meetings. This allows more freedom in location although the higher cost of trunk telephone calls to staff or computers has to be remembered. If raw materials and transport costs are of limited importance, the higher cost of staff in a city and their higher rate of turnover will be marked disadvantages. An urban location is also relatively less desirable now for polluting industries, given that the control of pollution has become a major concern of governments. Firms in cities are often required to invest heavily in equipment to reduce their factories' polluting discharges and this can add greatly to their overall costs of production. Less densely peopled areas may allow greater emissions of pollutants and hence be cheaper places to operate a factory. Encouraged by this, some firms are, therefore, moving their large-scale routine manufacturing operations to smaller towns where turnover of staff is less rapid, competition for labour less severe and land cheaper. Their upper management, research and sales departments may continue in the city enjoying its remaining advantages and making the strategic decisions, while the day-to-day management of the manufacturing process is delegated to middle management at the factory. The increasing separation of publishing in the city from printing elsewhere is a case in point. The separation of manufacturing and upper management is more practical for very large firms with many factories — which are increasingly dominant in western economies (see pp. 31–37).

For some industries, the savings come not so much from proximity to the city as from proximity to other firms making similar products. These savings, collectively termed localisation economies, take many forms depending on the industry concerned. In the jewellery trade the close physical proximity of firms may improve security and the swift dissemination of information about sharp practices. For the ladies' fashion trade nearness allows information to be acquired rapidly about new styles and a shared system for distributing clothes to customers is possible. For companies at the forefront of the electronics industry, nearness to other such companies is vital to learn of technical developments as quickly as possible and also for poaching talented designers and scientists from other companies. Localisation economies tend to be most marked for small firms. Large firms are more self-sufficient in terms of skill, information and trading links and so can generate these savings within their own organisations. They can be more independent of other firms when choosing where to operate.

Other firms require to be near companies to which they are functionally linked. Being near one's customers or suppliers may reduce distribution costs, particularly where the product is expensive to transport. The cluster of chemical companies around any oil refinery or of component manufacturers around a car-assembly plant are good examples of how the most important of these linkages can affect industrial location. Soviet economic planners have recognised the strength of these linkages and attempted to locate linked industries close to each other in 'territorial production complexes'. These are mostly found in Siberia and are described further in Hamilton's companion volume in this series *The Planned Economies*. The linkages between growing industries and the beneficial effects they have on a region's employment and incomes have also been used in the 'growth pole' concept in Western economies. This is discussed in more detail later (see pp. 24–25). Whereas some firms may gain by being close to related companies, others may find that their production costs are lower if they avoid the competition of rival firms by locating far away from them. They try to create a monopoly for themselves based on their distance from rival firms.

Conclusion

Since it costs money to produce any article and since the cost varies from place to place, it is reasonable for industrialists to locate their factories to minimise production costs. This presupposes, of course, that industrialists know how costs vary from place to place which may not be the case (see pp. 40–41). Once located, even the best factory site may become unsatisfactory as the distribution of costs, raw materials and technology alters. Relocation then becomes a possibility, but it is only beneficial if savings from the new site and the one-off costs of moving will outweigh any savings the firm could make by staying at its current site and changing its production methods, its suppliers or even the product made. Rather than relocating, a firm may switch to making an 'upmarket' version of its product which will have a higher profit margin, or to a new product where competition is less and again a higher profit margin is possible.

Exactly where the cheapest location is for any factory depends on its structure of costs. A general model, proposed by Scott, suggests that firms locate to minimise the cost of their most expensive input. In relation to a single city, the costs of the main requirements for industry vary as shown in figure 1. Firms needing expensive or large buildings (fixed capital) will locate in the suburban areas where land costs and rents are lower than in the central city. Alternatively firms requiring plenty of cheap labour will look either to inner-city areas or to rural areas. The countryside sometimes has the disadvantage of needing more working capital in the form of higher stocks of raw materials since deliveries are slower, particularly in larger countries like Canada and Australia rather than in the United Kingdom. The countryside is also a poorer place for the exchange of information. Therefore, inner-city areas attract manufacturing tasks which are unstandardised and hence resist mechanisation. They also have advantages for firms which must have rapid and frequent contacts

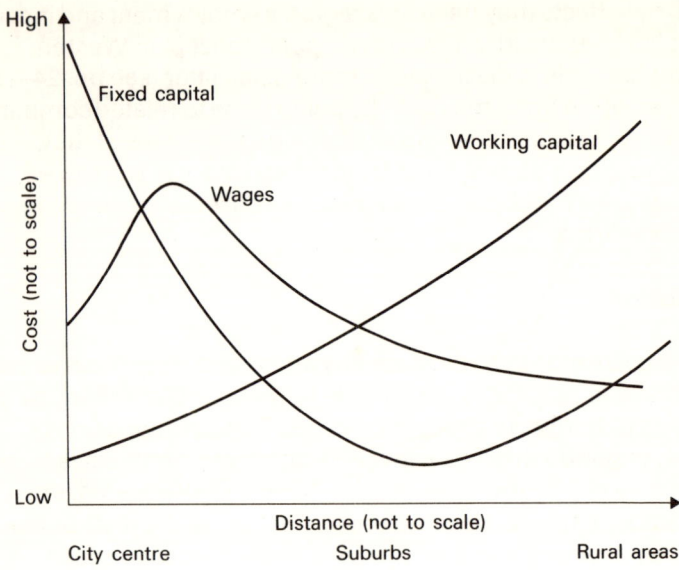

Figure 1 Current cost of factors of production in an urban area and its hinterland

with other firms and which need a great deal of labour. Inner-city areas tend to have an abundance of people prepared to work for lower wages such as the unskilled, immigrants and women. The prevalence of these groups in the city centre also partly reflects where cheap housing is to be found. Thus each firm should eventually locate in the part of the country where its combination of capital and labour costs will be minimised – the inner city has a comparative advantage for labour-intensive firms, the suburbs for capital-intensive ones.

A useful historical dimension can be incorporated into this model by noting that the distribution of costs within metropolitan areas is not static nor are firms' requirements constant (figure 2). The competition for land from office development has forced up land prices in city centres, while the substitution by many firms of capital in the form of large factories and machinery for labour has reduced the need they once had for cheap labour and increased their need for a cheap-land location. Competition between firms and the need to make adequate profits both reinforce this need for higher productivity from the employees through mechanisation. In this way, the decentralisation of the increasing numbers of capital-intensive firms from city centre to suburbs becomes entirely

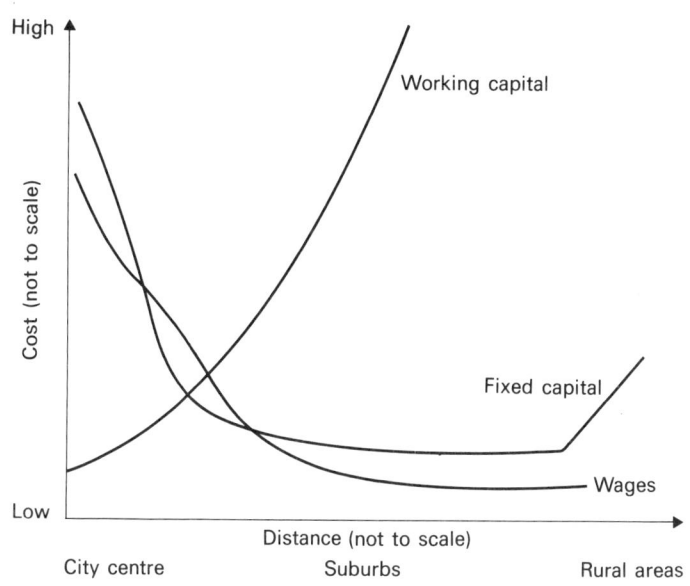

Figure 2 Cost of production c 1900 in an urban area and its hinterland

explicable just as does the decision of the remaining labour-intensive firms not to leave these areas. The process of decentralisation is unlikely to go on indefinitely since at some point the reduced industrial demand for labour and land in the city centre will so reduce land and labour costs there that, provided there is no other competition for these, some firms will be attracted back as the inner city regains some of its appeal and as wage rates climb higher in the suburbs. Decentralisation is likely therefore to create the conditions which will limit its continuation. Given the capital-intensive nature of the majority of modern industries, the suburbs are likely to have a comparative advantage over the city centre for some time to come, although for many industries rural areas may become relatively even more attractive in the future. Clearly the driving force in the location of industry as far as production costs are concerned is the changing character of industry and the demands firms make for land and labour. As these alter so the relative merits of different types of location must be reassessed.

Although production costs do affect where firms locate, they are not the only influence. The location of a firm may also affect the sales of its product and this relationship is examined in the next chapter.

11

Location and sales

In the previous chapter we examined how the location of a factory could affect the cost of manufacturing a product and hence influence the profitability of the company. Some places are cheaper locations than others for assembling raw materials and workers and creating a saleable product. The location of a factory may also affect the quantity and profitability of the product sold. Thus, a factory in the Yukon may sell less in the Canadian market than if it had been located in Toronto, for example. Location can affect sales in a number of ways. One way is where the demand for the product is highly concentrated. Luxury items tend to sell well in the largest cities where there is a relatively large number of wealthy people. Making *haute couture* clothes and jewellery, for example, in these large cities will also help sales because of the prestige (for which a higher price can be charged) of being based in New York or Paris rather than Scunthorpe or Wagga Wagga.

Another interesting approach to this topic is to consider the effects of the customers paying the cost of transporting the product from the factory to wherever they want to use it. The consequence of this is that the final price of the product rises as distance from the factory increases. So in figure 3 the customer at B has to pay more

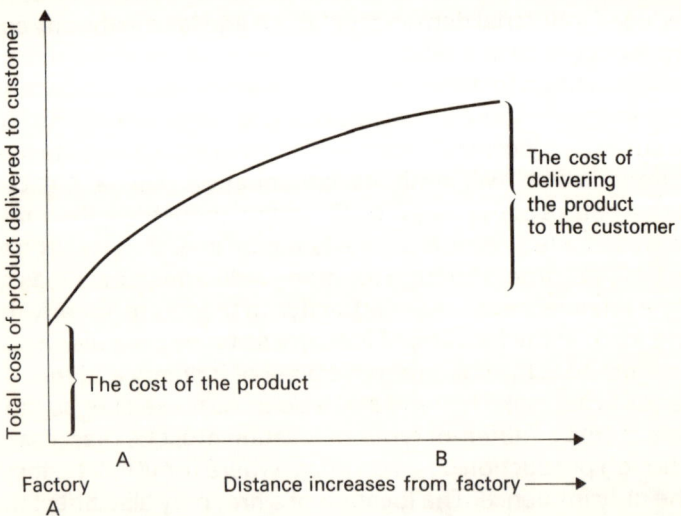

Figure 3 Effect of increasing distance from factory on delivered price of product

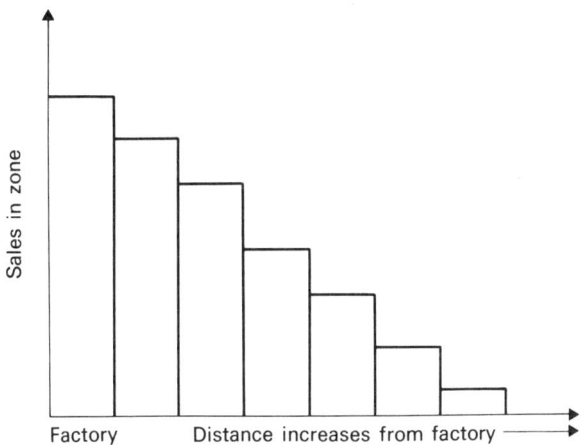

Figure 4 Effect of increasing distance from factory on sales

for the product than the customer at A and so is less likely to buy it. Therefore, sales will tend to decline as one moves away from the factory as figure 4 shows. There will come a point where the delivered price will rise so high that another firm will be able to supply the product more cheaply, as figure 5 shows. Even although the factory at A produces the product more cheaply – line Aa is

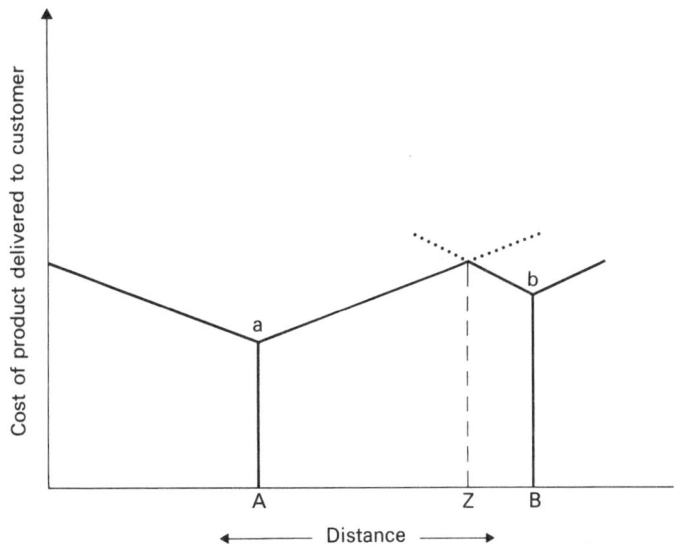

Figure 5 The market areas of factories at A and B

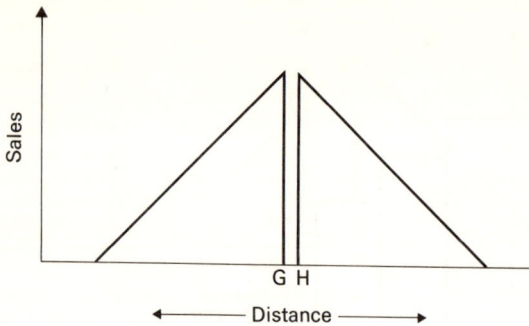

Figure 6 Two sellers located next to each other

shorter than line Bb – there still comes a point (here, Z) where the factory at B can supply the product more cheaply than A can. So the two factories have their own market areas, AZ and BZ. Each factory effectively has a monopoly over sales within its own market area because its price cannot be undercut.

An American economist, Hotelling, noted in 1929 how important for location this monopoly effect could be. Consider the case of the two salesmen at G and H in figure 6 who are selling the same product, say, ice cream on a beach. Unless people will buy ice cream irrespective of its cost, both sellers will lose sales to the left- and right-hand ends of the beach as greater costs and effort of travelling to and from the centre of the beach dissuade potential customers. However, both the salesmen will benefit if they locate as in figure 7, each gaining more customers at the margins of the beach then he loses at the centre. The salesmen must, of course, collaborate so as to reap this mutual benefit. So the best place for maximising sales (where these are sensitive to price) depends on whether firms in the industry collaborate or are independent and fiercely competitive. Collaboration will lead to a dispersal of factories each into its own market monopoly. Fierce competition may well lead to firms being closer together and having overlapping markets as each tries to force the other out of business. Only uncompetitive firms would seek peripheral areas with less competition so as to stave off bankruptcy.

In the real world, locating to maximise sales is actually a very difficult goal to achieve. Every change in the location of the customers means the firms in the industry ought to move too. Similarly, any change in the number of firms in the industry would

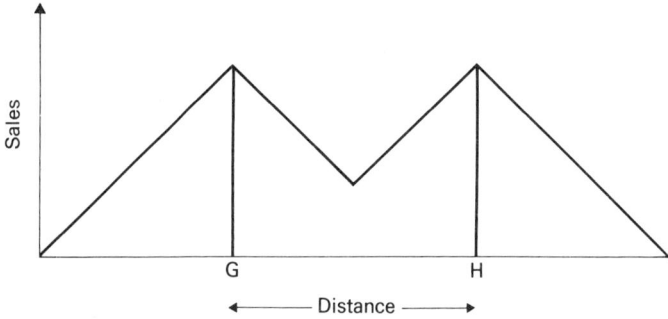

Figure 7 Two sellers located apart to gain marginal sales

require each existing firm to change location. Thus if firms enter an industry one at a time, the firm in figure 8a would have to move from its central location (which was ideal when it was the only firm) to a new position (figure 8b) when there were two firms. Similarly, if the number of firms increased to three or four (figures 8c and d) all the firms would have to move again to maintain their equal spatial monopolies. In real companies this would not happen so quickly, though some firms do move after their customers have relocated from city centre to suburbs, for example, or when competition from other firms has become too intense.

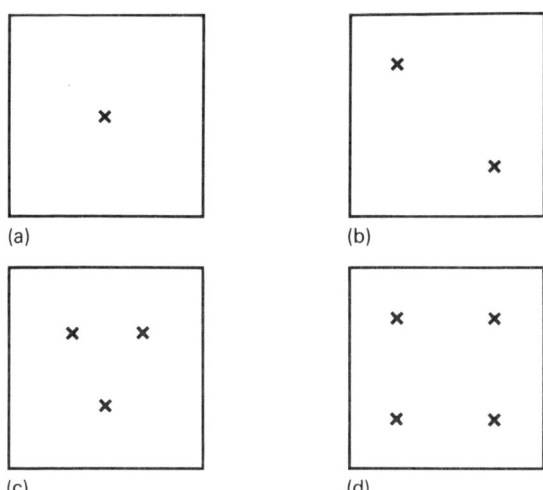

Figure 8 Relocation of firms to maintain equal spatial monopolies as the number of firms increases

However, this general rule applies only under certain circumstances. It assumes that transport to the customer forms a large part of the final price of the product to the customer. This may not be so for many products where transport is cheap. In such cases, competitors in widely separated factories may all be able to supply most of the market at similar prices now that transport is so much cheaper than formerly. Remoteness may no longer be a protection against competition. Indeed, for many products, the extra transport costs of selling to distant markets may be more than offset by the reduction in production costs by manufacturing more of the product. Many productive processes are of the type where increasing the volume of production reduces the cost of making each item. If it costs £10 per tonne to make steel in a small smelter, it may cost £7.50 a tonne in a medium-sized smelter working at full capacity and £6 per tonne in a large one at full capacity. In this case the extra transport costs of selling even a heavy item like steel to distant markets may be more than offset by the way extra output reduces production costs. This effect is important particularly for small economies. Many Third World countries only require limited quantities of refined oil, steel and consumer goods, for example, because they have small populations and are still at a low level of economic development. Locating a steel mill or refrigerator factory in the country would save on transport costs to the consumers, but this saving would be dwarfed by the higher cost of making the product in the small quantities the country needs. The history of much manufacturing industry has been for technical advances to raise the scale of production needed to minimise production costs for products like steel, cars and oil products. So the cost of entering many such industries is quite prohibitive without massive subsidies or import taxes to keep out the cheaper foreign products. The logic of reduced transport costs is to allow factories to spread out, while the logic of technical advance is to concentrate production in larger factories and export over increasing distances. It is a trend only national import taxes seem able to halt.

The effect of location on sales also depends on who pays for transporting the product to the consumer. So far in this chapter, it has been assumed that the customer pays this cost. This is what is known as f.o.b. (free-on-board) pricing. However, many firms now sell their goods using c.i.f. (cost, insurance, freight) pricing. Under the latter system, the product is sold at a single national price rather than at a separate price for each customer depending on his distance from the factory. C.i.f. pricing is, of course, administratively easier for the company and it has some important geographical consequences. For a company buying a product sold at a uniform price it does not matter where it locates in relation to its supplier. The cost of this raw material will be the same wherever it locates. So c.i.f. pricing means that items like the cost of labour or the cost of land rather than transport costs on raw materials affect production costs and location. However, for the company making the product, c.i.f. pricing does have a locational effect since a uniform price means, in effect, that customers near the factory pay more for the product so that distant customers may pay less. This system, which clearly raises sales in distant markets, will only work if there are a large number of nearby customers each paying a little more so that larger savings can be made for a smaller number of distant customers. Large increases in price to nearby customers would give an opportunity to competitors to steal the local market while ignoring the distant customers. Consequently c.i.f. pricing favours central locations near the heart of the market. It is also a subsidy to distant areas which helps them overcome the geographical fact of their greater distance from the heart of the economy. Some companies are half-way between the two types of pricing since they operate a zonal system of prices. Concentric zones are established around the factory. Within each zone there is one delivered price and the price rises in the zones further away from the factory. This zonal system is used by oil companies in setting the price of petrol in Great Britain, for example.

Pricing policy is also important where the market is not competitive but rather is a monopoly or cartel. In a monopoly, one company controls the sales of the product, while in a cartel (also called an oligopoly) a small number of companies combine to regulate the price of the product. In these circumstances, it is possible for the price to be much higher than the actual costs of manufacturing, transport and normal profits, in which case a location to maximise sales is not so vital unless the firm wants to make the largest possible profits. However, any monopoly has to be aware that competitors could be attracted to the industry if the sale price (and hence the company's profits) is too high. Monopolies usually survive either where one firm has control of an essential raw material or a piece of technical knowledge without which the product cannot be made or where the cost of entering the industry is prohibitively high. The system of patenting inventions helps to restrict the flow of information which may help foster monopolies. Cartels tend to be unstable unless there is some trust between the members. The fewer members there are in the cartel, the easier it is to hold together. The diamond market has been a relatively stable cartel for many years of, effectively, two members, the Soviet Union and the South African-based firm of De Beers. Similarly, the more expensive it is to find a substitute for the product in question, the stronger even a large cartel will be. The Organisation of Petroleum Exporting Countries (OPEC) is a good example of a large cartel which has held together for a remarkably long time because, in the short term, other countries must buy OPEC's oil.

Another way a cartel can affect prices, and hence sales, concerns the way transport costs may be manipulated to favour the companies in a particular area. The best known example of such a 'basing-point' system was the 'Pittsburgh plus' system used by steel manufacturers in Pittsburgh, USA. The arrangement was that steel sold anywhere in the United States was priced on the assumption that it had been transported to that place from Pittsburgh. The effect of this was that steel makers in the rest of the USA could not undercut Pittsburgh companies simply because they were nearer the customer. This was really a defensive measure by steel firms in Pittsburgh to maintain their control over the US steel market in the face of growing competition from low-cost manufacturers elsewhere such as in Birmingham, Alabama. The extent to which this system affected the location of the US steel industry is not clear but it certainly contributed to prolonging the dominance of the Pittsburgh area by reducing the sales of manufacturers elsewhere. Such control over the rates charged for transporting freight is only possible for very large companies in the absence of government regulation.

Today, major companies face a different locational problem which stems from the fact that they make many products. Where do you locate a factory which makes both lorries and cars when the markets for the two products may be in different areas? Even a factory making both large, expensive cars and small, cheap ones may find that the two markets are in different areas. Clearly, factories making several products will be located at a compromise site which is probably not ideal for maximising the sales of any one product but is reasonable for all of them.

Large companies have developed in another way which further alters the relationship between the location of their factories and sales. Large companies advertise. They create a demand for their product and increase sales above the level to be expected on the basis of price alone. Advertising may try to reduce the competition between a product and its rivals by creating a brand image which is unique. A higher price can then be charged and the location of the factory becomes less important. Often the brand image is an 'up market' one which seeks to sell at a higher price in return for the promise of a higher quality product. The British and American textile industries, faced with cheaper imports, are good examples of this. Marketing skills and stylish design can convert otherwise high-cost locations for textiles, like New England and Lancashire, into satisfactory ones.

Marketing also involves another important aspect of sales, namely a regional strategy. Often a company establishing a new product will have been involved in considerable outlay to equip the factory and buy stocks of raw materials. In order to recoup this outlay as quickly as possible, the product is sold first in the biggest market where salesmen can minimise the distance between customers. A fast build-up of sales is often an important goal for new firms with limited financial resources. Siting the factory in this core area for sales may also be useful for getting feedback from the early customers on how the product meets their needs and on how it and its components (perhaps also made locally) can be improved. Later, the market may be expanded to include other areas, perhaps even in other countries, but the factory will stay where initially established. Moving to a new site costs money, so unless the benefit from the new site through extra sales is considerable, the factory may remain at its original site which was excellent for initial sales even though it has subsequently become rather unsatisfactory.

Conclusion

So far, consideration has been given to the relationship between the location of a factory and the quantity of goods sold. It is not a simple relationship since it depends on who pays for transporting the product to the customer, whether it is a competitive industry and whether there are scale economies in production. Also important are the size of the local market, how many products are made at the factory and the effectiveness of the company's marketing and advertising. The discussion has also assumed that companies and customers are free to trade as they wish. In modern times this is no longer true since governments are increasingly seeking to influence where industry is sited, and it is this government influence which is explored in the next chapter.

Government influence

We have already examined some of the ways in which the free market affects industrial location. In most countries governments have tried to alter the distribution of industry produced by the free market so as to achieve a variety of economic and political objectives. This chapter will study the direct and indirect methods of influencing industrial location which local and national governments have used.

Direct control

Governments may wish to exert direct control over the location of certain industries for reasons of public safety. Factories which are heavily polluting or inherently dangerous may be located in remoter areas to protect the public. Nuclear power stations, explosives works and military experimental establishments fall into this category. Broader strategic considerations may also influence government policy. During the Second World War, for instance, the Soviet Union moved some of its industrial capacity east of the Urals and in Great Britain west-coast sites were similarly favoured. In both cases the aim was to distance the factories from Germany and protect them from air attack. The greater range of current military aircraft has eliminated the value of this in Europe, yet even today the legacy of industrial premises built in this period has a continuing influence on the distribution of industry.

Direct control is also exercised over the location of government's own factories. Most are concerned with manufacturing or testing military equipment or space technology and in some countries tobacco and distilling, for example, are state monopolies as well. Both civil and military research establishments are often run by the government and a concentration of these in the environs of the capital city is frequently evident. All but one of the British Ministry of Defence's thirty-two research and development establishments in 1975 were within 160 km of London. Employees of such establishments who set up their own businesses to exploit new military technologies will usually stay in the same area, so perpetuating the effects of government decisions on industrial location. The direct control of industrial location by communist governments as part of the centrally planned socialist economy is studied in detail in Hamilton's *The Planned Economies* in this series.

Individual companies may also find themselves in a position where government is able to control where they set up their activities. Industries which need government finance to develop expensive factories or which are dependent on government contracts or subsidies may be vulnerable to such pressure. Steel works, aluminium smelters and electronics companies are particularly liable to be instructed to locate in areas of high unemployment or for electoral advantage. Johnston has observed how Federal spending and contracts in the United States have been very unevenly distributed between states depending on the membership of Congressional committees. In another example of control over private companies, the British Government required two smaller steel works to be set up in different regions in the later 1950s rather than one very large mill which would have produced cheaper steel. This avoided the politically awkward decision of the siting of the one large mill. With two mills to site, two regions were appeased.

On a more detailed level local authorities often seek to control the location of new factories as part of their land-use planning. Areas are zoned for industry so as to protect residential areas from pollution or heavy traffic. Local authorities may also select the type of industry they allow into their area. The Isle of Man and the Channel Islands, for example, seek to attract only high technology, non-polluting industries which will not strain their limited labour supplies or affect the tourist trade.

Indirect control

In non-communist countries indirect control of industrial location is much more extensive than direct control. The most obvious example of indirect control is regional policy.

A regional policy is usually adopted because of the existence of marked regional variations in standards of living, as measured by criteria such as rates of unemployment, out-migration and low incomes. In some countries such regional disparities have been left to cure themselves on the assumption that high unemployment and consequently low wages will ultimately attract labour-intensive firms. The rapid industrialisation since 1960 of the southern states of the USA with their low wages and high unemployment is often cited as evidence of the effectiveness of *not* having a regional policy. The governments of other countries such as France, Italy and the United Kingdom have argued that, while market forces may in some circumstances remove the worst regional disparities in the long run, a well directed regional policy will often achieve this more quickly, with less suffering and less electoral danger from regional separatist movements.

Regional policy usually works indirectly since grants and subsidies are given to those firms wishing to set up in designated parts of the country. In the United Kindom these are called assisted areas. Firms are not usually forced to accept these grants, but it is argued that enough will accept the regional subsidy to bring about a redistribution of employment in manufacturing which will close the gap between richer and poorer regions. In some countries restrictions are also placed on firms in more prosperous regions such as south-east England or Paris, in order to prevent firms there expanding existing factories or setting up new ones. The enthusiasm for regional policy in the UK has varied over the years as figure 9 shows, the strong pursuit of regional policy being indicated by many refusals for factory development in the prosperous areas.

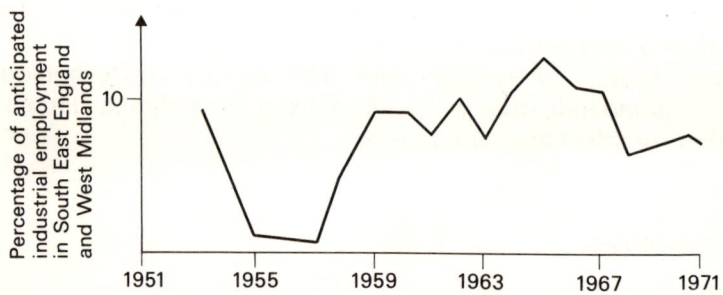

Figure 9 Employment diverted from south-east England and west Midlands by refusal of permission for factory development as a percentage of all anticipated industrial employment in these regions

Such periods are predominantly but not exclusively associated with Labour governments. Such a 'stick and carrot' approach of disincentives in some areas and subsidies in others should even out regional disparities and so make the management of the national economy easier. A given policy – reflation, for example, or a reduction in money supply – will then affect each region equally if they all start from the same level of economic health.

While the objectives of regional policy may seem clear, the means of achieving them have been the focus for considerable controversy. Incentives to establish factories can either be made available to large sections of the country or be restricted to small areas where investment in infrastructure will be concentrated. The former tactic is politically advantageous since many areas benefit from it and firms still have some freedom of choice of location. However, the tactic of concentrating aid is cheaper and allows assistance to be directed at those areas which need it most. Until recently, aid has tended to be given widely in the United Kingdom (figure 10).

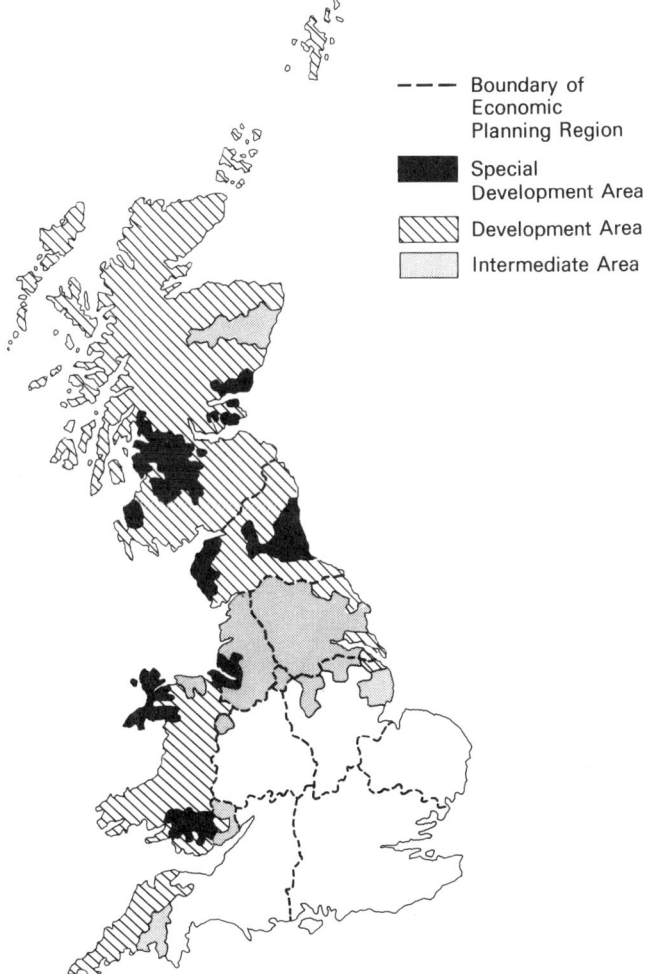

Figure 10 Assisted areas in Great Britain, November 1977

There has also been a parallel debate on the need for selectivity. In principle, aid can be given to any firm which wishes to move to an assisted area or only to firms meeting certain criteria regarding potential for employment, efficiency or the formation of links with other local firms. In the United Kingdom there has been a compromise, with additional help given during the last ten years to industries with growth potential (such as microelectronics) over and above the assistance available to most manufacturing firms.

A French economist, François Perroux, writing in 1950, recommended combining geographic and economic selectivity to form growth poles. A growth pole was a small area into which would be concentrated a rapidly expanding sector of the economy — electronics, for example. This concentration would lead, it was argued, to greater local spin-offs in terms of incomes and employment than if that industry were more widely dispersed across the nation. The tactic of designating growth poles has been used in Spain, France and Norway, while in Great Britain it was adopted in central Scotland (figure 11) and, less extensively, in north-east England. The main practical difficulty arose from attempting to convert the theoretical concept of a growth pole into a tool of practical industrial planning in specific regions. Proponents of growth poles have failed to agree about the optimum number of growth poles. Central Scotland had eight while the whole of Spain had only seven. The balance of political advantage clearly lies once

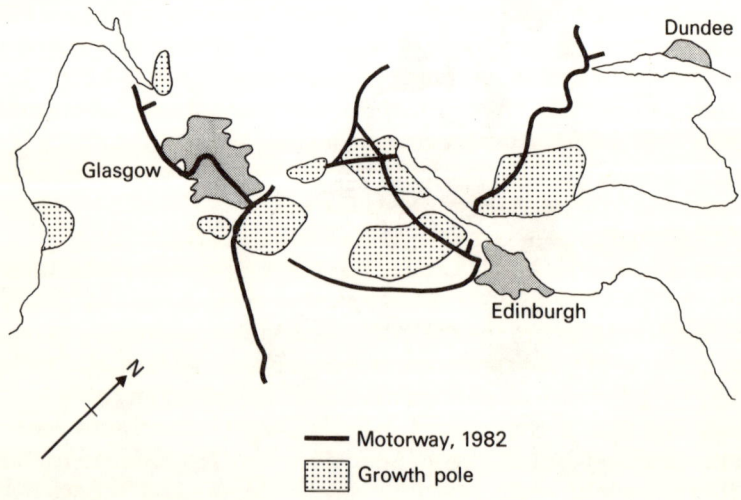

Figure 11 Growth poles in central Scotland

again in not being selective and so designating many growth poles. Neither was it clear whether a growth pole had to be based on a large city, nor whether it could be as small as an industrial estate. Finally, a growth pole implies selectivity but the theory provides no guidance on how to select the areas and industries with growth potential, particularly when costs and the demand for products are constantly evolving.

Regional policy may also be operated by means of two broad types of subsidies, those on the employment of labour and those on capital investment. Labour subsidies clearly encourage firms to employ more people and so they directly attack high unemployment. On the other hand, they also redistribute labour-intensive industries which often pay low wages and they may be an inducement to low labour productivity and over-manning. Subsidies on capital investment tend to lead to greater productive efficiency as well as orders for capital equipment and so they encourage a more modern manufacturing sector in the assisted areas. However, capital subsidies can lead to very heavy investment in capital-intensive industries which are highly automated and create few jobs. Oil refineries, for example, attract a great deal of subsidy since they are so expensive to build but they employ few people. Capital subsidies, which have been the main tool of regional policy in the United Kingdom, can be very expensive in terms of the cost to the government of each job created.

A cheaper alternative to subsidising the movement of industry is to subsidise the movement of unemployed workers to jobs outside their home area. Such a policy of labour mobility has always been a minor theme of British regional policy although it has been in operation since 1928. The cost to the government of each job created is lower than with the labour or capital subsidies, yet the policy is open to criticism of hastening the removal of the more skilled and enterprising from already depressed areas.

With all methods of regional policy the hardest question to answer is how effective the policy has been. How many jobs have been created which would not have existed without regional policy? How much smaller are the regional disparities in unemployment rates because of government control over industrial location? In the United Kingdom the disparities have been shrinking as Table 1 shows. The ratio of the rates of unemployment in the South-East and the assisted areas has also been declining. Regional policy has created extra jobs when used intensively – Moore and Rhodes estimated, perhaps optimistically, 260000 extra jobs in assisted areas between 1963 and 1970. Some argue that this has been at considerable cost to the public purse. Others suggest that the savings through not paying unemployment benefit and the greater revenue from income tax almost offset the cost of the subsidies.

Table 1 Declining regional disparities in the United Kingdom, 1966–80, in gross domestic product per head

	1966	1980
United Kingdom	100.0	100.0
Scotland	89.0	96.0
Wales	84.1	87.3
Northern Ireland	63.3	74.9

Currently it is being questioned whether British regional policy should be continued since, some argue, the problems of high unemployment and low incomes which formerly characterised whole regions are now urban problems, and particularly inner-city ones (figure 12). Consequently there has been some modest shift of emphasis by using the tools of regional policy in an urban context through inner-city partnerships and enterprise zones while withdrawing some or all regional aid from considerable parts of the country (figure 13).

Governments also achieve some indirect control over the location of industry through selective taxation and subsidies. A tax on oil imports which protects a domestic coal-mining industry will also affect the distribution of employment in mining by preventing pit closures. Imports of cotton textiles to the developed world are also taxed to bolster the home industry. National protectionism can also take the form of special grants to loss-making private companies (e.g. railways in the United States), or writing off the losses of wholly or partially nationalised concerns such as shipbuilding yards. More subtle forms of protection include favouring local companies over foreign suppliers for North Sea oil contracts and computers. The US Government requires that half of American overseas trade be carried in US-built and registered ships. By whatever means it is applied, the effect of protectionism is to maintain a more extensive industrial system within the nation's boundaries than would otherwise occur. Without protectionism there would either be less industrial employment or those who were employed would have obtained jobs in other industries. Both the nation's industrial structure and the geographical distribution of

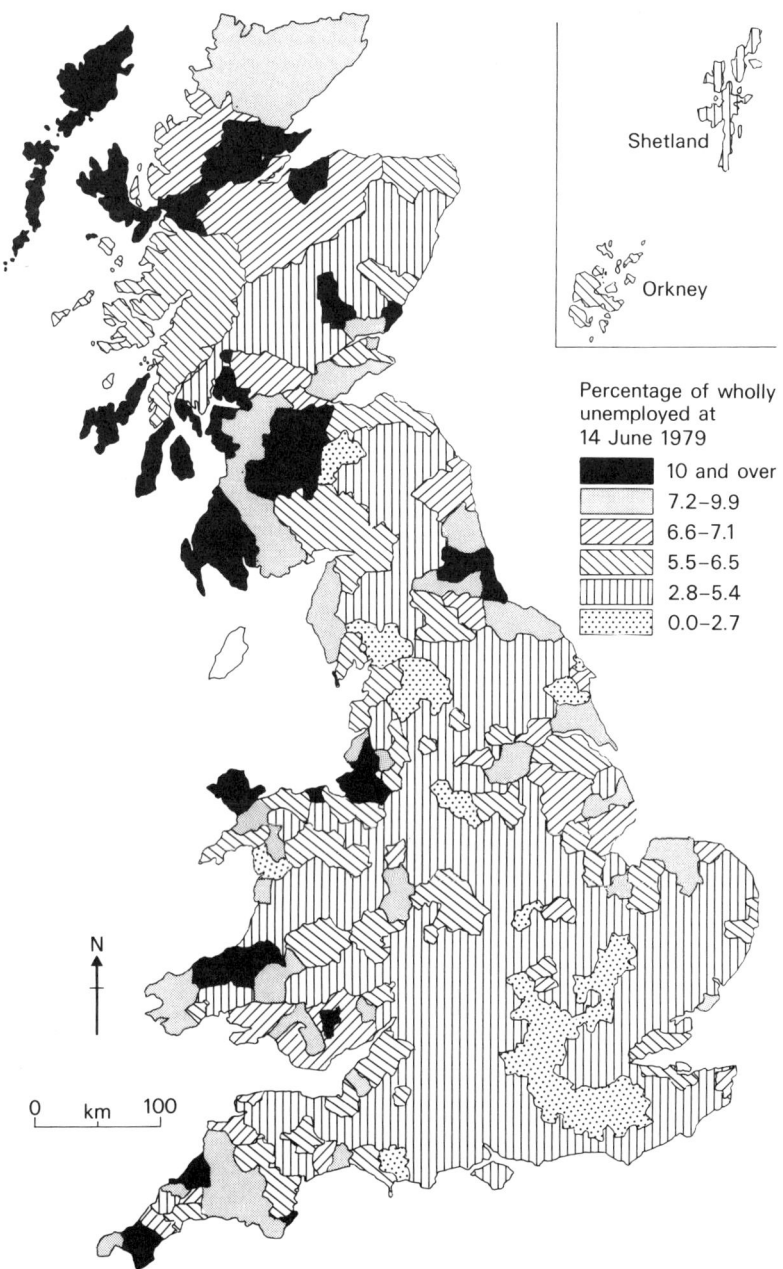

Figure 12 Percentage of work force wholly unemployed in Great Britain at June 1979

its population would have changed faster without protectionism. Government investment in a motorway network or a single gauge of railway network (as in Australia) may also affect industrial location

▲ Enterprise zone (March 1982)
△ Enterprise zone proposed in November 1982
● Inner-city partnership (March 1982)
▨ Area losing assisted area status or being downgraded

Figure 13 Enterprise zones, inner-city partnerships and areas losing assisted area status, 1980–82

by making it possible to supply a national market from a single central factory.

Indirect government control is also exercised by policies which are not specifically concerned to affect industrial location but which clearly have this result. High taxes on petrol and diesel fuel may be intended to conserve oil reserves or to raise revenue for the government, but they also implicitly favour urban over rural sites for factories. They favour central locations over peripheral ones for firms with national markets and they provide a degree of protection against competition for firms with local markets where transport costs are a major consideration. Extensive investment in fast railways and motorways has the opposite effect of allowing national markets to be served from a single factory.

Environmental policy can also affect the distribution of industry. The setting of environmental standards – through, for example, the Environmental Protection Act in the United States – encouraged polluting firms to locate in the cleaner areas, where their discharges would not breach the environmental standard, rather than in the areas already polluted heavily and above the standard. Environmental standards may therefore spread pollution more widely while curtailing its worst excesses. In a world of multinational companies which can play off governments against each other, the attraction of industrial investment from overseas and the maintenance of high environmental standards may be incompatible.

Conclusion

Government influence on the location of industry can be summarised as being characterised by four main features. First, it is difficult to measure its effects since what would have happened in the absence of any government policy is a matter of conjecture. Second, there is considerable inertia in government industrial policy. Once established, it acquires supporters with vested interests in its continuance even when the policy has arguably lost its effectiveness. Third, government influence on industrial location is unpredictable in its effects since the various branches of government have a variety of objectives, such as rapid growth of the economy, reduced government spending, low inflation or fairness between different social groups. Sometimes several mutually exclusive objectives are being pursued simultaneously so that the detail of policy may fluctuate unpredictably as first one and then another objective is given prominence. A final characteristic of government influence is the not infrequent lack of coordination between its various aspects as they are implemented through taxation, local planning, industrial subsidies and the general management of the national economy. However, none of these features detracts from the fact that governments are a potent, if selective and unpredictable influence on where manufacturing industry is located.

The structure of industry

In the previous chapters we examined the general influence on industry of spatial variations in production costs and sales, and also the effect of government policy on industrial location. Industry was treated in these chapters as a single entity since all firms have to consider how their location will affect what they pay for their raw materials and how much of the finished article they sell. However, firms differ not only in what they produce, but also in their size and the way they are organised.

Some sectors of the economy are dominated by small firms – the manufacture of furniture, for example – while in others large firms control most of the production. Examples of the latter include the motor car industry and computer manufacture where the public are willing to buy standardised products manufactured on a large scale. The trend in most countries, and particularly in the United Kingdom and the United States, has been for large firms to expand at the expense of smaller ones. In 1900 the one hundred largest firms in Britain were responsible for about 15 per cent of the net output of British manufacturing. Today they account for nearly a half. Some firms like the oil companies have largely grown because of good management and an expanding demand for their products. For others, like British Leyland and ICI, take-overs and mergers with existing companies have been an important method of growth, while for a third group of firms expansion was caused by nationalisation. As an indication of the size of these very large companies, only twenty-two countries in the world had gross national products in 1977 greater than the sales income of the oil company, Exxon, which is the largest American company. By whichever means these large companies have grown, their immense size changes the way they view the question of where they should manufacture their products.

Such large companies are sometimes able to alter some of the basic assumptions which lie behind the analysis of industrial location to be found in the first two chapters. They may be so large that they do not compete in terms of selling price with the few other companies in their field. In this case the incentive to find a location which will minimise production costs or maximise sales revenue is effectively blunted. Because of the scale of their purchases of raw materials, they may be able to influence the prices they pay for their raw materials, which smaller companies cannot do to the same extent. Even national governments may be willing to meet the requirements of such companies in order to attract the jobs and foreign exchange earnings a major new factory can bring. Whereas small companies have to accept their business environment as they find it and survive by adapting their way of working to its constraints, very large companies can alter their business environment to some extent so that it more nearly meets their needs for security, growth and profitability. This chapter will explore in more detail how large companies locate their factories.

Monopolies

If one company is the only supplier of a product for which there are no substitutes, then that company is said to be a monopoly. Monopolies are rare and short-lived in the private sector because raw materials and the requisite technology are usually available to more than one company. In theory, a monopoly could charge whatever it wished for its products. However, this would have to be tempered by the need to keep prices low so as to avoid losing sales which are sensitive to price. A monopoly for an absolutely essential product with no substitutes, like salt, would be ideal for a company. Unfortunately, in this case every coastline provides a potential source of supply for rival firms. Monopolies also have to be aware that if their prices are too far above the minimum possible, competitors could be attracted into the industry to undercut them. So even a firm which was the only supplier of a product would have to consider the potential of a good factory location for helping to minimise production costs and maximise sales. The threat of competition and loss of sales will mean that the advantages of different locations will still have to be assessed in the conventional manner, even if the lack of actual competition allows the company to disregard minor weaknesses in the siting of its factories.

Most monopolies today are found in the public sector rather than in private industry. Nationalisation often creates state monopolies particularly in the supply of services such as gas, electricity, water and telecommunications. Nationalisation of manufacturing industry is less common and often competition from home or overseas private companies making the same product forces the state company to view location seriously. However, the critical point is whether the state monopoly is subject to strict financial control by its government. If it is, efficiency and profitability must be maintained and it will be continually re-assessing its locational requirements.

If financial control is lax, locational inertia will prevail. Old sites inherited often from pre-nationalisation private companies will continue to be used despite their higher running costs.

If the central government does decide to simulate the effect of competition on a state monopoly by refusing to allow it to lose money, then a new political dimension comes into play. If some sites are no longer ideal, which should close and where should new investment be placed? State monopolies are usually more sensitive than private companies to the social and political consequences of decisions to build or close factories. Consequently, they often try to preserve the regional distribution of the industry, replacing jobs in old works with those in new factories. The rationalisation of the state-owned British steel industry, for example, attempted to concentrate the production of each steel-making area into a few new mills while closing old ones. Few steel-making areas received no new investment even though in strictly commercial terms this might be justifiable.

Cartels

It is much more common for a small number of companies, rather than just one, to control the production of a sector of the economy. This is called a cartel or oligopoly. The temptation is for the companies to cooperate or collude to suppress competition, though this may be disguised since it is illegal in most countries. They may divide up a country into market areas for each firm as British cement companies used to do. Alternatively, they can control the selling price of the product, as British motor car companies did in the 1970s and American steel companies based in Pittsburgh did in the 1920s. In one, perhaps extreme, case the British steel industry before it was nationalised operated a fund which received money from the low-cost producers of steel which was re-distributed to high-cost producers. The group of companies subsidised each other to prevent bankruptcies and so maintain the distribution of steel-making in the face of changes in production costs and sales which would otherwise have created a much faster relocation of steel works to coastal sites.

Large firms in Great Britain have usually expanded principally by means of mergers and take-overs rather than by their own internal growth. Sometimes this has been encouraged by the government so as to increase international competitiveness, for example in the heavy electrical engineering sector. In the United States, intense merger activity in the late nineteenth century provoked 'anti-trust' legislation which has hindered mergers and encouraged internal growth as a method of expansion. A merger places a company in an interesting position since it acquires at a stroke one or more factories located by an entirely different organisation with different needs and resources. After the merger, all the factories may continue to produce the same goods or some may be closed as production is 'rationalised'.

Two geographers, Leigh and North, studied a range of take-overs and concluded that their effects were complex. Nearly all involved some transfer of managerial control from the acquired factory to the new headquarters. The larger the company, the more likely it was to have its headquarters in south-east England, particularly London. Eighty-eight of the hundred largest British manufacturing firms in 1972 had their headquarters in London. So the distribution of the control of factories is increasingly concentrated in London and the other major cities of the world because of takeovers. However, the amount of control lost by an acquired factory varies depending on the parent company's knowledge of its activities. In the clothing sector, factories tend to remain relatively autonomous since only they have the detailed understanding of their products' styles and marketing. Conversely, autonomy is low in the chemical sector since the parent company has the skills to control all but the day-to-day operations. Autonomy tends to be greater where a firm is diversifying (for example, a tobacco company taking over a food company) and so lacks initially the expertise to run the new enterprise.

In about half the take-overs they examined, the acquired factory increased its output after take-over. Firms often want to be taken over so as to gain new secure markets and capital for expansion. They see take-overs as a good way to secure supplies of raw materials or outlets for their products.

Another result of a take-over is that a factory is closed. Low-profit lines are discontinued, production is concentrated at one large works, usually the most modern, and is shut down at other older plants which are often in the inner city. The growth through mergers and take-overs of a small number of major brewing companies in the United Kingdom since 1945 has been accompanied by a concentration of brewing in a few large modern breweries. The economies possible through large-scale production of a few standardised products outweighed higher distribution costs. Plant closure is commonest where sales of the product are falling or where technical advance is so fast that labour productivity is rising more quickly than the demand for the product. In either case, the market can be supplied using fewer workers and factories.

Occasionally, firms buy factories to suppress competition deliberately or simply to acquire the land, which may have development potential for offices or housing. In this case, the firm has no interest in the manufacturing process and the factory, often on an inner-city site, may be closed soon after take-over. This is sometimes known as 'asset-stripping'.

Branch plants

So far we have considered the range of effects of taking over existing factories. However, large companies also set up new factories of their own. This may be because they are starting production of a new item and a new site would be cheaper than any of their existing ones for this product. Cheaper labour may attract these branch factories to low-wage areas in depressed regions such as Scotland, the southern states of the USA or the Far East. This is particularly noticeable in sectors where wages form a large part of total costs, such as textiles, shoe manufacture or assembly-line work. A branch plant overseas may also avoid the taxes which would be due on imports from the parent factory. American companies which entered the European market after 1945 set up factories in Britain, France and West Germany so as to avoid import taxes in these countries on goods produced in the USA. The general reduction in import tariffs throughout the world under the General Agreement on Tariffs and Trade (GATT) and the formation of free-trade areas such as the European Economic Community (EEC) have reduced the need for factories in each country. One factory in the EEC may be enough to supply the whole West European market now that there are fewer barriers to trade between the member states. The advantage has swung to central locations within the EEC particularly when the company applies uniform pricing (see pp. 16–17) and even south-east England is peripheral in this situation. This is a clear example of how taxation policy can affect the international distribution of industry and of how small an item transport costs now are for most goods in relation to the economies possible by operating a single, very large factory.

Branch plants tend to be associated with expansion and with new products which have reached that stage of development where their manufacture has become a routine process. The development of new products, research and major financial functions tend to remain at or near the headquarters of companies. There are those who argue that branch plants are essential to the economic health of regions with industries persistently declining in employment like coal, shipbuilding and textiles. They provide jobs in areas of high unemployment and diversify the industrial base of the region making it less susceptible to the fortunes of a few products. Research also suggests that branch plants are not as liable to be shut down as the popular view of them would lead one to believe. They also tend to bring in that hallmark of a successful multinational company – efficient, if tough management. On the other hand, it can be argued that they stifle other firms by buying little from the local economy. Their sources of raw materials, markets and white-collar services usually come from the parent company, even when it is quite distant. They also tend to make fewer demands on the skills of the local workforce through assembly-line work, for example, which reduces wage rates, and they usually employ fewer technical, professional and managerial staff since their headquarters supplies these services. There is also evidence that some multinational companies manipulate the prices at which they transfer goods between their subsidiaries in different countries so as to artificially make losses in countries with high company taxation and large profits in low-taxation countries. Some host countries may thus be denied their fair share of the companies' profits by this 'transfer pricing'. There is a lively controversy over the extent of this strategem among multinational companies.

Branch plants are not an unmixed blessing, particularly in the longer term, but often they are all that areas of high unemployment can get. In some regions they dominate the economy, particularly in Third World countries but also in parts of the developed world such as the Netherlands, Canada, Northern Ireland and central Scotland. In the United Kingdom, the foreign-controlled workforce increased in size by 71.7 per cent between 1963 and 1975 whereas employment in domestic manufacturing firms declined by 13.5 per cent. The greatest power of the multinational company is that it can affect the relative economic attractiveness of places. It can play off governments against each other so that they will compete to offer even bigger incentives to locate in one country rather than another. It can borrow from banks at lower rates of interest than can smaller companies and it can either force along the pace of technical change (which may mean closing factories making old products and establishing new ones in different places) or it can try to stifle competition.

The large company is therefore partly freed from its economic environment. It does not have to take costs and selling prices as fixed constraints within which it has to work. It can change the demand for products and it can alter its economic environment by advertising and innovation which will change people's preferences and propensity to spend. The effect of this on the geography of industry is to concentrate into fewer hands the power to mould the economic future of regions and countries. Decisions taken on another continent about what to produce and whether to compete with other companies will open or close whole factories. Financial problems in one part of a multinational company may have repercussions on factories in other countries making other products. Therefore changes in the structure of industry have tended to integrate the world economy but to lessen the links between factories next door to each other.

The precise effects of the trend to larger companies will also depend on whether their objectives are the same as those of the small businessmen on whom the classical location theory in Chapters 1 and 2 is based. If the large private company uses its dominance in the market to suppress competition, perpetuate old products, buy out competitors and seek agreements for 'orderly marketing', then large companies are a conservative force in industrial location. They tend to preserve the *status quo* of where factories are located, what they make and how they are linked to their suppliers and customers. If, however, large companies do compete on price and innovate, they have the resources to be a powerful force for rapid change. The logic for that change will not lie in the individual factory nor even in the locality in which it is situated. Rather it will lie in the rest of the organisation of which the factory is a small part. How multinational and other large companies use their power will vary from company to company – large companies are a diverse group with different markets, resources and goals. Nevertheless, a loss of local control over industrial development is the principal effect of the growth of very large manufacturing enterprises.

The influence of industrialists

Those geographers and economists who have studied the distribution of industry have always appreciated that industrialists were the people who finally decided where to site production. What has changed during the last twenty years is the importance attached to their influence. It used to be argued that the pattern and logic of industrial location was derived solely from large-scale economic and political forces acting on manufacturing firms. An individual industrialist might occasionally choose to ignore these forces and if he did, he would either go out of business, or have to tolerate lower profits or adapt his business methods. Whatever the outcome, the result was of no more than curiosity value as a demonstration of human irrationality. More recently attitudes among researchers have changed as it has been appreciated that the influence of industrialists was neither minor, irrational nor random. Such influence has become the focus of a considerable research effort which has clarified greatly our understanding of industrial location.

The study of industrialists as people with minds of their own has increased the links between industrial geography and psychology and it has been accompanied by a considerable amount of fieldwork as case studies or samples of industrialists have been studied. The work has tended to focus on three topics.
1 Businessmen's aims
2 Businessmen's information
3 Altering businessmen's information
This chapter will explore these three areas.

Businessmen's aims

The classical theories of industrial location described in the first two chapters were based on the assumption that businessmen had one objective, namely to make the largest possible profits. In order to do this it was necessary for them to either maximise sales revenue, minimise production costs or, preferably, do both. This immediately raises two questions.

First, what is the rational response when maximising profits in the short term requires a different location from profit maximisation in the long term? It is not unreasonable to assume that the dynamism of technological change, population growth and changing transport technology will alter the best location for a factory. Hence short-term and long-term views may lead the businessman into different courses of action. How far ahead do businessmen plan? Research so far on this important question has been sparse but it would seem as though the uncertainty of the future leads industrialists either to inaction or into behaving as though the future will be similar to the present even for investments with a long working life. Hence, short-term solutions are more common than long-term ones, particularly for smaller companies.

The second question concerns whether profit maximisation, over whatever span of time, is what industrialists are aiming to achieve. An American economist, Simon, drew attention in 1959 to the important distinction between how businessmen ought to behave in order to maximise the benefit their business brings to themselves and the national economy, and how they actually behave. He noted that businessmen have many objectives rather than just one. They may want a combination of growth, prestige, safety, profits, an easy time or a challenge. Achieving any one of these goals may be possible in a static world, but to achieve many of them in a rapidly changing one is clearly impossible.

Simon's view can be summarised in three propositions. First, businessmen do not know how to maximise profits. Second, as the managers rather than the owners (that is, the shareholders) of companies, they would not benefit from profit maximisation even if they could achieve it, and so have no incentive to follow this course. Third, businessmen are concerned to use their limited skills and information to achieve acceptable results from running the company. Therefore, a satisfactory site is what they seek, not an ideal one.

This begs the question of what precisely 'satisfactory' means. For many businessmen it implies avoiding risks and the possibility of losing money. This may mean that the important point is to avoid locating in certain types of places rather than being attracted to particularly desirable sites. Areas to be avoided would include those with an unattractive environment, poor labour relations or a small population and unreliable markets. Avoiding risks rather than seeking out the maximum advantage also favours a city location over one in a smaller settlement. Part of the explanation for the continuing attractiveness of cities for industry lies in the security they provide as much as in the measurable financial advantages they possess. They offer numerous alternatives in terms of methods of transport, power supplies, markets, suppliers and services like banks and advertising agencies. If any of these proves inadequate or breaks down, other sources and the widest range of service industries can be brought into use rapidly. Only cities, and especially the larger cities, can provide such security. This is as important an advantage for a place to possess as any other in a situation where businessmen are trying to pursue many different, perhaps even incompatible objectives in a rapidly changing world full of uncertainties and pitfalls.

Businessmen's information

The classical location theories presented in the first two chapters can only operate if each industrialist has complete and accurate information about costs and prices and how they vary spatially. Only this information can allow the calculation of the optimum location for a factory. In the real world, businessmen are no nearer omniscience than anyone else. Information takes time to assemble and time is expensive. Townroe's study in 1972 of businesses which moved premises or set up new factories showed that thorough and extensive searches for sites were a feature only of large branch plants which had important links with the parent plant or where there were major technological requirements for the site. Forced moves of factories tended to be towards suboptimal sites since time was a severe constraint preventing a thorough search for the best alternative. He also noted that decisions made by committee rather than by a single individual tended to be more consistent to a set of locational criteria for a suitable site. However, he concluded that all locational decisions, even in the largest companies and for major new factories were to some extent suboptimal. This is partly due to the fact that the information businessmen do have tends to be out of date and partial. Brown has shown how firms which moved from inner to outer London tended to stay in the same sector of the city. Basildon, for example, to the east of London, attracted firms from the eastern sector of inner London, whereas firms decentralising to Crawley which is south of London, came from the southern sector of inner London. This sectoral narrowing down of the area in which to search for a new factory is aided by the radial pattern of roads and public transport in most cities.

Businessmen also make poor locational decisions since most of them are faced very infrequently with the need to find a new site. It is not a common task which, with experience, can be carried out in an increasingly efficient and thorough way. Except in the largest companies, most businessmen are too busy with other tasks to give their full attention to all the work needed to assess the best new site for a factory. The temptation is considerable to rely on partial information, stereotypes of places and 'common sense'. This way a decision can be reached quickly without getting 'bogged down in detail'. Ignorance, therefore, is a good tool for rapid decision-making so that other managerial tasks can be taken on.

If businessmen are not as knowledgeable, perhaps deliberately, about the economic environment as they ought to be, then on what basis do they take locational decisions? Out-of-date information plays a part, as do preconceived ideas based on the common image of places — 'rainy', 'go-ahead', 'poor industrial relations', 'classy' or 'down-at-heel', for example. These stereotypes can be used to narrow down the area of search for a new location, particularly in the smaller companies. The outdated information upon which stereotypes are based is also important because of its role in forecasting. Any commercial decision which involves a programme of investment must be based on a forecast of the returns on that investment in the future and hence on a forecast of the prospective economic situation. Studies of how people make forecasts show that most forecasts are conservative in the sense that they are biased towards a future more like the immediate past than usually turns out. People are reluctant to make forecasts involving a marked change from the present. Uncertainty is a powerful force for the *status quo* stifling major changes in the location of industry. Therefore the inertia which perpetuates industrial regions may be due as much to the geographical conservatism of businessmen as to any real advantages in the current distribution of industry.

Altering businessmen's knowledge

The distribution of industry is of obvious importance to the firms but it is also important for towns and cities. A firm can bring employment and so enhance local incomes. If unemployment is high, it is worth the community's attempting to put its case before the companies so they will be aware of the community's advantages for industry. This is a sensible tactic for educating businessmen provided only a few locations are advertising themselves. If many localities promote themselves, the impact of each is diminished by the babble of newspaper advertisements and literature posted to companies. Each community becomes a product to be packaged, caricatured or otherwise made to seem attractive. Yet although the benefits from an advertising campaign are difficult to measure, stopping advertising runs the risk of losing potential jobs to other areas. Because of the high cost of advertising much of it is done by regional and national governments, particularly on an international scale. Media advertising, 'hospitality', promotional campaigns and study visits arranged by diplomatic staff overseas are all methods used. Other tactics used to persuade companies include visits to factories from that country already established in the area and appeals to the, for example, Scottish or Irish ancestry of American executives so they will locate in these countries.

Since advertising is expensive, local authorities attempt to promote those aspects of the area which research on industrial location suggests will make an impact on industrialists. The availability of premises, government grants, centrality and access to motorways, docks and airports are claimed by nearly every town and region, often using maps and diagrams to boost their case. The quality of the environment is stressed in prose and photographs particularly as this relates to housing, schools and shopping facilities. The easy access to the countryside and sports facilities is often mentioned. Another tactic is to cite the well-known companies which have already moved into the area, hoping that this will induce a 'follow my leader' reaction among other firms anxious to avoid taking risks. Despite the heavy cost of advertising widely, there is a remarkable similarity to the advertisements of many towns, each using the others' tactics in case that is the one which will sway businessmen toward their area. In recessionary times advertising sometimes seems like a lifebelt to areas with high unemployment even if they are not quite sure how to use it (figure 14).

The study of how businessmen make decisions on where to locate factories is still in its infancy but enough has been discovered to show that this is an important aspect of the subject. It is certainly not a random or irrational influence. The future seems to lie in integrating the study of decision-making with the growth of multi-national corporations discussed above in 'The structure of industry'. How decisions are made by large companies producing many items and running factories in several countries is likely to be a complex but vital area of future study. Investigations are also needed into the effectiveness of government influence on businessmen which was discussed above in 'Government influence' (pp. 20–30). As an example, one study in 1977 by Green showed a marked ignorance, particularly in small firms, of the incentives offered by the British Government under its regional policy. The critical questions are about how much information businessmen have and how they interpret it.

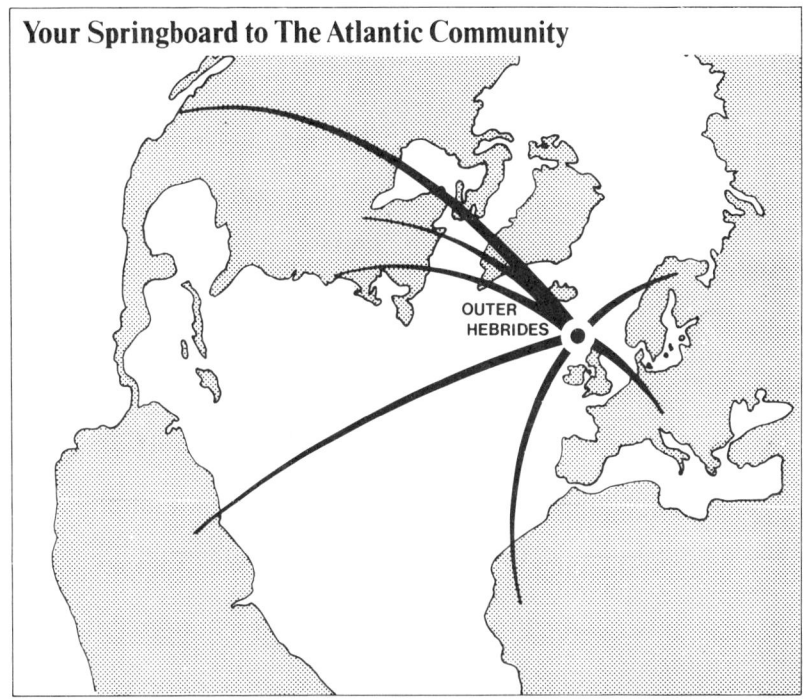

Thinking of setting up a new factory?

Well, think about the Outer Hebrides – your springboard to the whole of the North Atlantic. We're at the heart of shipping lanes to so many places. And travel within the Outer Hebrides is easy too – quiet roads and three airports all waiting to serve *you* and only 90 minutes from London.

The islands are your dream come true – romantic moors, friendly people and an unhurried way of life that is ideal for bringing up a family. A loyal well-trained workforce is waiting for you.

Why not come and join over 50 other companies in the Outer Hebrides – there's plenty of space and unbelievably low rents.

The Outer Hebrides – your springboard to the Atlantic Community.

Figure 14 An imaginary advertisement for industrial promotion in the Outer Hebrides

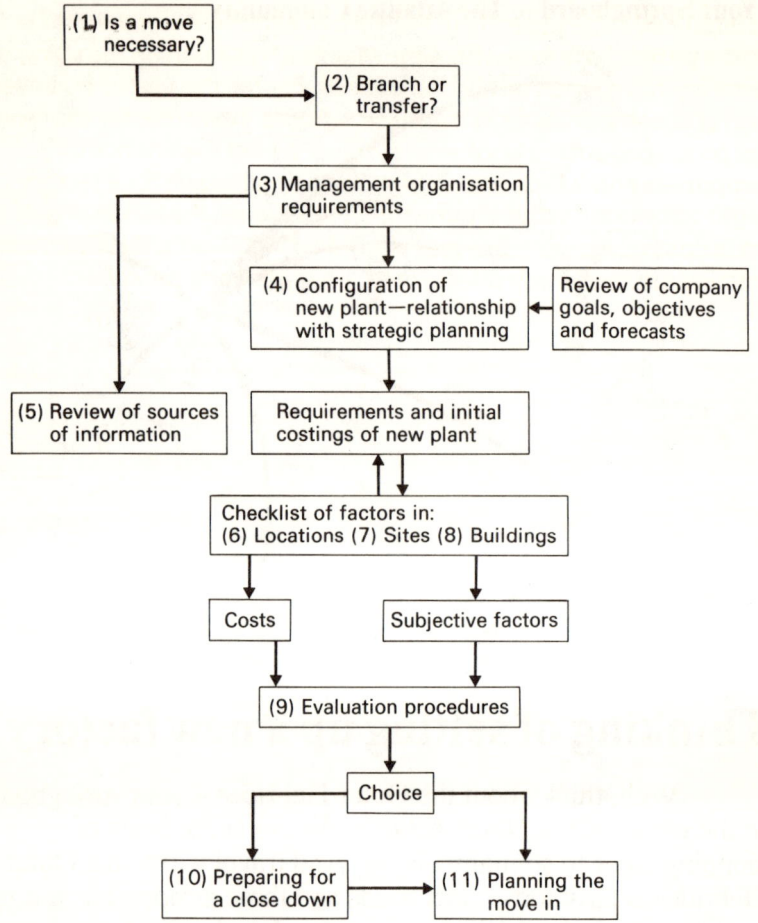

Figure 15 How businessmen are taught to choose a factory site (after Townroe, 1976)

Similarly investigations are needed into how much importance businessmen attach to a locational decision. Is it regarded as a major strategic decision upon which a substantial part of the company's future success lies, or is it viewed as a minor administrative matter? The difficulty with all these sorts of questions lies in unravelling industrialists' real reasons for their actions, particularly when they are part of a committee structure, from the reasons they subsequently believe they had at the time or believe they ought to have had. Decisions are frequently rationalised subsequently in the light of experience and training. This is particularly true where the results of research on the siting of factories have been published specifically for the use of businessmen and companies or in business schools. Townroe, for example, has produced such a book which draws on the experience of companies and which shows how choosing the site for a factory ought to be conducted (figure 15). In this sense, the rationality of the industrial location process should be increasing. Research and practice are becoming intertwined, each affecting the other.

Conclusion

The distribution of industry reflects the nature of the economy. The last one hundred years have witnessed the economies of North America and Western Europe changing from domination by farming, first to domination by manufacturing, and then to the kinds of economy we find today where manufacturing is being replaced rapidly by the service (tertiary) sector as the principal source of employment. The same period has witnessed the replacement of small-scale capitalism by economies dominated by very large companies and with substantial nationalised sectors. Government policy in most countries has evolved from a *laissez-faire* approach, with very limited government interference in the workings of industry, to one of considerable control even in the free-market economies of the USA and Japan.

These changes have affected the distribution of industry. National markets have replaced local ones for most firms and international markets are common even for medium-sized firms. Transport costs are usually so low relative to other manufacturing costs that distant suppliers and customers are possible, particularly when uniform pricing is employed. The growth of multinational companies has added a new dimension to industrial location. Each factory is operated not only to manufacture products profitably but also to play its part in the company as a whole. The establishment and operation of such a factory can only be understood in relation to the spectrum of the company's activities.

Another important change has been in the role of competition. Free competition between firms was the driving force behind the location theories presented in the first two chapters. Firms constantly sought to minimise production costs and maximise sales in order to survive, and the correct location for the factory had a major part to play in achieving these objectives. Today, free competition has allowed the emergence of a few, very large companies which dominate many sectors of the economy. Sometimes these firms are restricted by legislation attempting to preserve free competition and prevent monopolies developing. More often, these firms work closely with central government as the spearhead of the country's export drive. Very large companies do not always compete so vigorously as small compaies. Collusion or at least 'cooperation' becomes possible. The contradiction inherent in free competition is that it cannot survive since some companies by luck, skill and good location are better at it than others.

Yet for the large companies there is still a driving force spurring them on to change. Today that driving force is no longer free competition, it is labour productivity. Production costs still need to be reduced and, since transport costs are so low, the major item for most firms is wages. Therefore the paramount needs are to reduce the amount of labour required by means of mechanisation and automation, and to pay the remaining workforce less by using less skilled labour or moving production to a low-wage area. Of course, if many companies set up in a low-wage area (Hong Kong in the 1950s for example) wages will rise and the firms will have to move up-market as they are undercut by even lower-wage areas elsewhere in south-east Asia. Therefore there is still a dynamic quality to industrial location. Firms are looking for different qualities in places and the places themselves are changing in the qualities they have to offer industrialists. One result may be that industry is still attracted to the same areas as before – cities, for example, albeit further out from the inner city than before. However, the reasons for industrialists choosing cities may be rather different. The city no longer has a monopoly of skilled labour, rapid communications and nearby markets. Today it provides a rapid supply of raw materials, which saves money by allowing smaller stocks to be kept, and it is generally a low-risk location since such a variety of skills, contacts and markets are potentially available quickly.

Another effect of the change to a multinational capitalism is the increasing ability of firms to affect their economic environment. Previously, firms either found the right place for their activities, or they modified their activities so that they fitted in with the qualities of their chosen location. Today, firms can modify aspects of places so that they will meet their needs more fully. They may be able to alter the level of government grants. They can get discounts on their raw materials and transport costs. Therefore the relationship between firms and places is a reflexive one now. Each alters the other.

There is also a sense in which publications like this book affect industrial location. As more and more potential businessmen are trained at school, university or business school to be managers, so they read the results of research on other companies and they learn about theories of industrial location. They come to feel that that is how firms ought to be located. Therefore the publication of books about industrial location, which seek to show how orderly and rational the process is, tend to educate the next generation of businessmen in how they ought to go about setting up factories. It is arguable that research on industrial location has tended to make the process more rational, or at least to make businessmen feel they ought to do it rationally, even if it is not always so in practice. In effect, the research becomes a self-fulfilling prophecy.

Two further points are worth bearing in mind about industrial location. Although it is an important process for firms and for regional and national economies, it remains only one of many areas where the managers of companies have to make decisions. It has to be seen, if possible, in its broader context of the firms' objectives and their other activities. Very often, the interesting feature of the locations of factories is why they do *not* change. Since moving a factory is expensive, it is interesting to study all the other changes which are made to help survive a poor location.

The other point to consider is that industrial location will never be fully predictable. No single theory can be envisaged which could explain precisely why all factories are sited as they were, let alone forecast all future locations. The most that one can do is to explain the broad pattern and the major influences and trends. Partly this is because of the uncertainty inherent in an economy. One does not know how prices will alter or government policy evolve. The average businessman does not have the time to research these matters sufficiently to minimise his lack of knowledge, so he relies on his hopes, fears, prejudices, half-formed notions and guesses. Yet even so, as the chapter on 'The influence of industrialists' showed, the location of industry is neither a random process, since general trends can be detected, nor is it irrational.

Studying the distribution of manufacturing is a complex part of human geography and one where everyone, businessman and geographer, is learning. The former is learning to make better locational decisions; the latter to understand businessmen more clearly and to grasp the forces acting to alter the distribution of industry. It is a process we need to understand both at a personal level and as a facet of the evolution of the world economy. If it is to be controlled, for whatever purpose, then it has to be understood and this book has attempted to assist that process.

Topics for discussion

1 One of the features of the last fifty years has been the relative decline in the cost of transporting goods. Do you think this is likely to continue? Suppose the cost of transporting goods were to double in the next twelve months due to severe increases in the price of oil. What short-term and long-term effects would this have on the distribution of industry?
2 How does the government assist the development of industry in the United Kingdom and in any other countries you are studying?
3 By examining newspapers, periodicals and any other sources you can find, describe the way governments and industrial promotion agencies try to change the image of places so as to attract industrialists.
4 How have the creation and successive enlargements of the European Economic Community affected the location of industry?
5 Is it possible to have a theory of industrial location?
6 If 'industrial location is a reflection of the nature of the economy', how is industrial location likely to change during the next twenty-five years in (a) the United Kingdom (b) the United States of America (c) any Third World country you have studied?

Further reading

P.E. Lloyd and P. Dicken, *Location in Space*, Harper and Row, 1977. An extensive review of the topics of this book.

F. E. I. Hamilton (ed.), *Industrial Change – International Experience and Public Policy*, Longman, 1978.

R. C. Estall and R. O. Buchanan, *Industrial Activity and Economic Geography*, Hutchinson, 3rd edn., 1973. A clear and basic introduction.

D. M. Smith, *Industrial Location*, Wiley, 2nd edn., 1981. A useful companion to Chapters 1 and 2.

F. E. I. Hamilton, *Models of Industrial Location*, pp. 361–424 in R. J. Chorley and P. Haggett (eds.) *Models in Geography*, Methuen, 1967. Concerned with theories of industrial location.

D. Keeble, *Industrial Location and Planning in the United Kingdom*, Methuen, 1976.

G. C. Cameron (ed.), *The Future of the British Conurbations*, Longman, 1980, Chapters 1–3, 5, 10 and 11. Discusses the geography of industry in British cities.

D. MacLennan and J. B. Parr, *Regional Policy – Past Experience and New Directions*, Martin Robertson, 1979.

C. F. Carter and B. R. Williams, *Investment in Innovation*, Macdonald, 1971. Does not deal specifically with industrial location but an excellent guide to the concerns and aims of businessmen.

Acknowledgements

The author and publishers wish to thank the following who have kindly given permission for the use of copyright material:

Front cover   Aerofilms
Figure 11   HMSO, Scottish Development Department, *Central Scotland – a programme for development and growth*, Cmnd 2188, 1963, Edinburgh
Figure 12   A. R. Townsend, *Factors in the Geography of Unemployment Evident in the British Government's Map of Regional Aid*, Paper to the Annual Conference of the Institute of British Geographers, 1980.

The author would like to acknowledge the assistance of Mrs Christine Skinner and Miss Carolyn Brown who typed drafts of the text and of Mrs Marian Jackson who proof-read the text.